BEAUTY
& HARMONY

In the Words of 'Abdu'l-Bahá

BAHÁ'Í
PUBLISHING

WILMETTE, ILLINOIS

Bahá'í Publishing
401 Greenleaf Avenue, Wilmette, Illinois 60091
Copyright © 2021 by the National Spiritual Assembly
of the Bahá'ís of the United States
All rights reserved. Published 2021

Printed in the United States of America on acid-free paper ∞
24   23   22   21   4   3   2   1

ISBN 978-1-61851-197-3

Cover design by Carlos Esparza
Book design by Patrick Falso

Extracts 3, 5, 20 are from *Selections from the Writings of 'Abdu'l-Bahá*.
Wilmette, IL: Bahá'í Publishing, 2010.

Extracts 7, 13, 25 are from *Some Answered Questions*.
Haifa: Bahá'í World Centre, 2014.

Extract 27 is from *'Abdu'l-Bahá in London: Addresses and Notes of Conversations*.
London: Bahá'í Publishing Trust, 1982.

Extracts 6, 11, 15, 16, 19, 21, 23, 26, 28 are from *Paris Talks: Addresses Given by 'Abdu'l-Bahá in Paris in 1911*. Wilmette, IL: Bahá'í Publishing, 2011.

Extracts 1, 2, 4, 8, 9, 10, 12, 14, 17, 18, 22, 24 are from *The Promulgation of Universal Peace: Talks Delivered by 'Abdu'l-Bahá during His Visit to the United States and Canada in 1912*. Wilmette, IL: Bahá'í Publishing, 2012.

'Abdu'l-Bahá

November 2021 will mark the hundredth anniversary of the passing of a figure beloved by many. 'Abdu'l-Bahá, meaning *Servant of the Glory*, is the title assumed by Abbás Effendi (1844–1921), the son and appointed successor of Bahá'u'lláh—the Prophet and Founder of the Bahá'í Faith. 'Abdu'l-Bahá shared a lifetime of exile with his Father at the hands of the Persian and Ottoman Empires, and was a prisoner for forty years. Despite the severe hardships that characterized his life, he dedicated his energy to the service of others and radiated joy and selfless contentment at all times. His charitable deeds and undiscriminating love for all are well documented in the accounts of countless souls who crossed his path, and his timeless and deep wisdom is recorded extensively in both his written works and in the transcripts of his many public addresses. He is known by Bahá'ís as the perfect exemplar of the Faith's teachings.

1

The composite beauty of humanity will be witnessed in their unity and blending. How glorious the spectacle of real unity among mankind! How conducive to peace, confidence and happiness if races and nations were united in fellowship and accord! The Prophets of God were sent into the world upon this mission of unity and agreement: that these long-separated sheep might flock together.

2

The worlds of God are in perfect harmony and correspondence one with another. Each world in this limitless universe is, as it were, a mirror reflecting the history and nature of all the rest. The physical universe is, likewise, in perfect correspondence with the spiritual or divine realm. The world of matter is an outer expression or facsimile of the inner kingdom of spirit. The world of minds corresponds with the world of hearts.

3

Strive with heart and soul in order to bring about union and harmony among the white and the black and prove thereby the unity of the Bahá'í world wherein distinction of color findeth no place, but where hearts only are considered.

4

Religion must reconcile and be in harmony with science and reason. If the religious beliefs of mankind are contrary to science and opposed to reason, they are none other than superstitions and without divine authority, for the Lord God has endowed man with the faculty of reason in order that through its exercise he may arrive at the verities of existence. Reason is the discoverer of the realities of things, and that which conflicts with its conclusions is the product of human fancy and imagination.

5

. . . in this new age the Manifest Light hath, in His holy Tablets, specifically proclaimed that music, sung or played, is spiritual food for soul and heart.

The musician's art is among those arts worthy of the highest praise, and it moveth the hearts of all who grieve. Wherefore . . . play and sing out the holy words of God with wondrous tones in the gatherings of the friends, that the listener may be freed from chains of care and sorrow, and his soul may leap for joy and humble itself in prayer to the realm of Glory.

6

Behold a beautiful garden full of flowers, shrubs, and trees. Each flower has a different charm, a peculiar beauty, its own delicious perfume and beautiful color. The trees too, how varied are they in size, in growth, in foliage—and what different fruits they bear! Yet all these flowers, shrubs and trees spring from the self-same earth, the same sun shines upon them and the same clouds give them rain.

So it is with humanity. It is made up of many races, and its peoples are of different color, white, black, yellow, brown and red—but they all come from the same God, and all are servants to Him.

7

. . . in this wondrous Dispensation the earth will become another earth and the world of humanity will be arrayed with perfect composure and adornment. Strife, contention, and bloodshed will give way to peace, sincerity, and harmony. Among the nations, peoples, kindreds, and governments, love and amity will prevail and cooperation and close connection will be firmly established.

8

Do you appreciate the Day in which you live?

This is the century of the Blessed Perfection!

This is the cycle of the light of His beauty!

This is the consummate day of all the Prophets!

These are the days of seed sowing. These are the days of tree planting. The bountiful bestowals of God are successive. He who sows a seed in this day will behold his reward in the fruits and harvest of the heavenly Kingdom. This timely seed, when planted in the hearts of the beloved of God, will be watered by showers of divine mercy and warmed by the sunshine of divine love. Its fruitage and flower shall be the solidarity of mankind, the perfection of justice and the praiseworthy attributes of heaven manifest in humanity.

9

The world of humanity, too, is like a garden, and humankind are like the many-colored flowers. Therefore, different colors constitute an adornment. In the same way, there are many colors in the realm of animals. Doves are of many colors; nevertheless, they live in utmost harmony. They never look at color; instead, they look at the species. How often white doves fly with black ones. In the same way, other birds and varicolored animals never look at color; they look at the species.

Now ponder this: Animals, despite the fact that they lack reason and understanding, do not make colors the cause of conflict. Why should man, who has reason, create conflict? This is wholly unworthy of him.

10

Bahá'u'lláh declared that religion is in complete harmony with science and reason. If religious belief and doctrine is at variance with reason, it proceeds from the limited mind of man and not from God; therefore, it is unworthy of belief and not deserving of attention; the heart finds no rest in it, and real faith is impossible. How can man believe that which he knows to be opposed to reason? Is this possible? Can the heart accept that which reason denies? Reason is the first faculty of man, and the religion of God is in harmony with it.

11

Thoughts of war bring destruction to all harmony, well-being, restfulness and content.

Thoughts of love are constructive of brotherhood, peace, friendship, and happiness.

12

If the oneness of the human world were established, all the differences which separate mankind would be eradicated. Strife and warfare would cease, and the world of humanity would find repose. Universal peace would be promoted, and the East and West would be conjoined in a strong bond. All men would be sheltered beneath one tabernacle. Native lands would become one; races and religions would be unified. The people of the world would live together in harmony, and their well-being would be assured.

13

[The] universal Manifestation will subdue the world through a spiritual power, not through war and strife. He will array the world with peace and harmony, not with swords and spears. He will establish this divine sovereignty through genuine love, not through military might. He will promote these divine teachings through kindness and amity, not through violence and arms.

14

Considering this wonderful unity of the kingdoms of existence and their embodiment in the highest and noblest creature, why should man be at variance and in conflict with man? Is it fitting and justifiable that he should be at war, when harmony and interdependence characterize the kingdoms of phenomenal life below him? The elements and lower organisms are synchronized in the great plan of life. Shall man, infinitely above them in degree, be antagonistic and a destroyer of that perfection? God forbid such a condition!

From the fellowship and commingling of the elemental atoms life results. In their harmony and blending there is ever newness of existence. It is radiance, completeness; it is consummation; it is life itself. Just now the physical energies and natural forces which come under our immediate observation are all at peace. The sun is at peace with the earth upon which it shines. The soft breathing winds are at peace with the trees. All the elements are in harmony and equilibrium.

15

Put all your beliefs into harmony with science; there can be no opposition, for truth is one. When religion, shorn of its superstitions, traditions, and unintelligent dogmas, shows its conformity with science, then will there be a great unifying, cleansing force in the world which will sweep before it all wars, disagreements, discords and struggles—and then will mankind be united in the power of the Love of God.

16

God never forsakes His children who strive and work and pray! Let your hearts be filled with the strenuous desire that tranquility and harmony may encircle all this warring world. So will success crown your efforts, and with the universal brotherhood will come the Kingdom of God in peace and goodwill.

17

. . . we must ever strive for capacity and seek readiness. As long as we lack susceptibility, the beauties and bounties of God cannot penetrate.

18

My hope is that the white and the black will be united in perfect love and fellowship, with complete unity and brotherhood. Associate with each other, think of each other, and be like a rose garden. Anyone who goes into a rose garden will see various roses, white, pink, yellow, red, all growing together and replete with adornment. Each one accentuates the beauty of the other. Were all of one color, the garden would be monotonous to the eye. If they were all white or yellow or red, the garden would lack variety and attractiveness; but when the colors are varied, white, pink, yellow, red, there will be the greatest beauty. Therefore, I hope that you will be like a rose garden.

19

The diversity in the human family should be the cause of love and harmony, as it is in music where many different notes blend together in the making of a perfect chord. If you meet those of different race and color from yourself, do not mistrust them and withdraw yourself into your shell of conventionality, but rather be glad and show them kindness. Think of them as different colored roses growing in the beautiful garden of humanity, and rejoice to be among them.

20

The Abhá Beauty endured the most afflictive of calamities. He bore countless agonies and ills. He enjoyed not a moment's peace, drew not an easeful breath. He wandered, homeless, over desert sands and mountain slopes; He was shut in a fortress, and a prison cell. But to Him, His pauper's mat of straw was an eternal throne of glory, and His heavy chains a sovereign's carcanet. By day, by night, He lived under a whirring sword, and He was ready from moment to moment for death on the cross. He bore all this that He might purify the world, and deck it out with the tender mercies of the Lord God; that He might set it at rest; that conflict and aggression might be put to flight, the lance and the keen blade be exchanged for loving fellowship, malevolence and war turn into safety and gentleness and love. . . .

21

Light is good in whatsoever lamp it is burning! A rose is beautiful in whatsoever garden it may bloom! A star has the same radiance if it shines from the East or from the West. Be free from prejudice, so will you love the Sun of Truth from whatsoever point in the horizon it may arise!

22

Material civilization is like unto the lamp, while spiritual civilization is the light in that lamp. If the material and spiritual civilization become united, then we will have the light and the lamp together, and the outcome will be perfect. For material civilization is like unto a beautiful body, and spiritual civilization is like unto the spirit of life. If that wondrous spirit of life enters this beautiful body, the body will become a channel for the distribution and development of the perfections of humanity.

23

. . . love is attained through the knowledge of God, so that men see the Divine Love reflected in the heart. Each sees in the other the Beauty of God reflected in the soul, and finding this point of similarity, they are attracted to one another in love. This love will make all men the waves of one sea, this love will make them all the stars of one heaven and the fruits of one tree. This love will bring the realization of true accord, the foundation of real unity.

24

. . . when the spring comes, the showers descend, the sun floods the meadows and plains with light; you will observe creation clad in a new robe of expression. The showers have made the meadows green and verdant. . . . The spring has resuscitated all phenomena and has adorned the earth with beauty as it willeth.

Even so is the spiritual springtime when it comes. When the holy, divine Manifestations or Prophets appear in the world, a cycle of radiance, an age of mercy dawns. Everything is renewed. Minds, hearts and all human forces are reformed, perfections are quickened, sciences, discoveries and investigations are stimulated afresh, and everything appertaining to the virtues of the human world is revitalized.

25

. . . in the sight of God knowledge is the greatest human virtue and the noblest human perfection. To oppose knowledge is pure ignorance, and he who abhors knowledge and learning is not a human being but a mindless animal. For knowledge is light, life, felicity, perfection, and beauty, and causes the soul to draw nigh to the divine threshold. It is the honour and glory of the human realm and the greatest of God's bounties.

26

When perfect justice reigns in every country of the Eastern and Western World, then will the earth become a place of beauty. The dignity and equality of every servant of God will be acknowledged; the ideal of the solidarity of the human race, the true brotherhood of man, will be realized; and the glorious light of the Sun of Truth will illumine the souls of all men.

27

This is a brilliant century. Eyes are now open to the beauty of the oneness of humanity, of love and of brotherhood. The darkness of suppression will disappear and the light of unity will shine. We cannot bring love and unity to pass merely by talking of it. Knowledge is not enough. Wealth, science, education are good, we know: but we must also work and study to bring to maturity the fruit of knowledge.

28

Much of the discord and disunion of the world is created by these man-made oppositions and contradictions. If religion were in harmony with science and they walked together, much of the hatred and bitterness now bringing misery to the human race would be at an end.